The Buddhacarita

A Modern Sequel

The Poetic Saga of Buddha's Life

Tai Sheridan

Tai Sheridan

ISBN: 979-8-9899002-7-5
Print Edition

Tai Sheridan
1240 W Sims PMB 113
Port Townsend WA 98368

www.taisheridan.com
tai@taisheridan.com

Praise for Buddha in Blue Jeans

A single page gives such a gift that I take in my breath and am drawn to stop and take it in.

The simplest things are always the most precious. Tai Sheridan has shown this to be true.

Tai Sheridan delivers quality books over and over. This is one of them, enjoy. Short and sweet as ever.

Concise, accessible, remarkable. Seems like everything we need to know is found in these pages.

All of Tai's books are straight to the point Zen at its best.

Wisdom stripped to its bare bones.

This is one of the most basic yet insightful books I have read on Buddhism. It is a good short read for anyone with a serious life-threatening illness.

Read This!! This will blow your socks off! Simple as that!

If there were a higher rating to grant this small taste of beauty and reality, I would grant it.
Mindfulness at its peak.

You can pick up any of his books, flip them open to any page, and find inspiration.

Heart-awakening. Written with simplicity and clarity.

This poetic meditation on death is a wonderful gem.

I absolutely love this book and all of Tai Sheridan's writing.

Clear and kind, it calls me to simple things that make a big difference.

This is a very accessible and immediately essential book, filled with prayers anyone can use.

When sorrows come, they come not single spies, but in battalions.

- Shakespeare

It is better to conquer yourself than to win a thousand battles.

- Buddha

Dedication

To the storytellers
Who makes the sun sing
And the moon dance

&

To the sages
Who open their minds
And hearts to the world

Contents

Tai Sheridan

Introduction

The Buddhacarita, which is a Sanskrit poem written by Asvaghosa in the second century, is the oldest known story of the life of Buddha. The narrative begins with the magical birth of Prince Siddhartha and concludes with his enlightenment. This ancient myth depicts Buddha's unwavering quest for knowledge about the nature of reality. The story combines a hero's journey, Buddhist philosophy, historical facts, and fantastical elements.

I have created a modern sequel while remaining true to the original storyline and many of the original images. However, I transformed the structure into seven-line stanzas to imbue it with enchantment and lyricism. The rhyme scheme and alliteration are reminiscent of olden times. The original English translations are scholarly linguistic interpretations are difficult to read. This poetic version of The Buddhacarita deviates from the literal translations, but it is my hope that the poetic license used will bring joy and meaning to the modern reader

Tai Sheridan
Port Townsend
2024

Tai Sheridan

Canto 1: The Birth of Siddhartha

Sing sway shout heavenly praise
Celebrate for baby Buddha is born
His luminous lofty body raised
Bringing benefit to beings forlorn
Smashing surly darkness asunder
A sparkling sun a trembling thunder
Exquisite as the moon

The preeminent prince of magic place
White widespread with cumulus clouds
Spires palaces touching sky's lace
Royal rulers righteous noble proud
The townsfolk warmly issuing smiles
Everybody rich sans pride or guile
Ruby rainbows on Kailasa

A festival feast for Buddha's birth
Arched portals blossoms in abundance
Pinnacles atop pyramids of golden girth
Lapis lazuli and diamond substance
Great gods' minds now gathering awe
The Shakya clan's pride they foresaw
A rapturous regal tableau

Sunbeams shinning on golden palaces
Songs streamers banners displayed
The auspicious legacy in lofting breezes
The light of liberation all piously prayed
Dancing and reveling in hued moonlight
Celebrating the noble prince's birthright
Water-lilied silver pavilions

Sun oh radiating regal virile progenitor
Reclining retired from arduous toil
Amorously aroused by garment garter
Or lotus faced women daubed with oil
Their scintillating faces like the moon
Potent sun sprinting to western lagoons
Cooling lustful desires

Praise king of kings father Suddhodana
His lineage interlacing golden sun
Himself a herald of empty vistas
A liberal liege not arrogant baron
Empowering everyone to be complete
Each ennobled by his true heartbeat
A virtuous kindly leader

Suddhodana supporting the dharma flag
A natural nadir of the ten directions
Trumpeting emptiness like a mountain stag
Transcendent truths the dearest doctrines
To inward insight a rich heart awakens
Leave off self clinging the certain cannon
Blessings beyond appearance

King Suddhodana shimmered in light
Like fall's full moon pale and vast
With blackened backdrop a starry night
He queried Queen Maya after repast
Enter most gracious queen of queens
Sparkling splendor Suddhodana gleaned
Sun freed from darkness

Queen Maya great mother of all
Eminent glorious goddess to the world
Nourishing each with a mother's mistral
Blowing equally unfettered unfurled
A cow of plenty her essence glowed
A glad goddess in the king's abode
Heart of great devotion

From Tushita heaven the bodhisattva fell

Filament of past and present and future
Entering Maya's womb within to dwell
As a white elephant a six tusk trumpeter
Trampling tens of thousand of harms
The world wardens followed in swarms
Protecting the great bodhisattva

Queen Maya felt cadenced contractions
And with attendants approached the birth
In Lumbini's luscious garden as if heaven
Swaying from baobab bough in mirth
Her womb waters gushing a lily lotus
The babe born bare and mindfully zealous
To nobly walk earth

Queen Maya's vows plainly purified her
The heralded holy birth ensued sans pain
A valiant vibrant boy of golden glamour
The suffering of six worlds he'd arraign
Like the sun signaling through cinereal clouds
Darkness would no earth wonders enshroud
The world resplendent light

His glory grander than fall's new moon
Upon the momentous anointed arrival

Thousand-eyed Indra a cradled cocoon
Swaddling the palace prince most cheerful
Two clear shinning streams flowed
Down from highest heavenly abode
Showering mandara flowers

The regal prince born planted in wisdom
All worldly foolishness flung aside
His pure primal mind touching true freedom
In contemplative care did resolutely abide
After perfect progression in Maya's womb
Fine limbs lustrous as if heaven assumed
He was earth's sun

The prince permeated voluminous space
In glorious grandeur rendered beatific
All eyes espied his handsome face
A bright beaming sun or moonlit fabric
His mindful manner dissolving all self nature
His diamond body outshining a butter
Lamp's luminous hues

The boy strode seven slow solid steps
Alive like a buddha with lions gait
Spontaneously flowing sans moment's prep

Manifold meanings did his roar emanate
I am born of supreme knowledge purled
And am here for the welfare of the world
This is my last birth

The gods in homage hailed Maya's son
Holding up white umbrellas in limitless sky
Though hovering Himalayas were earth's apron
The world shook like ships tossed awry
Lotuses lavishly rained from cerulean blue
Breezes blew heavenly clothes askew
Sun gleaming gentle luster

Abruptly from air a pure well appeared
About the ancient women's quarters
Barren trees blossomed single and tiered
Fruity fragrance wafting from arbors
Sweet songs trilled lutes tambours drums
Female bees flew with bewildered hums
Snakes inhaled perfumed air

Multifold miracles as fathers surpassed sons
Valmak sang poetry across grassy acres
Where seer Cyayana's verses coarsened
And Arti's son molded medicinal ethers

His famed father could not imagine
Kueika's son dwelled in divine passion
Brahmanhood's sacred knowledge

King Suddhodana filled on splendid joy
From palace rooms and blissful wishes
Deleterious doubts at last destroyed
The prince proclaimed in songs speeches
The king transmitted treasures of worth
Honoring his wellspring ruler of earth
Long rule the prince

Sage Asita heard a voice most heavenly
On the path of charmed celestial beings
That in Kapila a king's son born wisely
For the sake of supreme spiritual blessings
As the sage contemplated sacred import
Away to the Sakya's palace he did transport
Indra's banner the prince

Acclaimed Asita arrived at the palace
Having heard through heavenly inspiration
Of a pleasing prince with liberating prowess
For destroying all birth and self notion
The sincere King saying he's Asita's disciple

Kindly asking for diverse directions ample
Regarding his newborn son

The sage spoke deep solemn words
His clear eyes wide with wonder
Your son will lead humans homewards
As is worthy of you great-souled elder
Lofty liberal and lover of divine duty
Your nature age wisdom truly trusty
Your heritage noble

The king taking the prince from nurse
Stumbled joyfully toward the holy sage
Asita let his gaze discover and disperse
Watching a wheel on wisdom's foot as presage
Seeing webbed fingers toes celestial marks
Entwined eyebrow hair in circular arc
Buddha's auspicious signs

Asita trickled tears on elegant eyelashes
Sighing and skyward looking to heaven
At which the anxious king hushes
Lest the privileged prince's fate darken
Then the kindly king with hands in prayer
Sobbing with love requested an answer

Tai Sheridan

From the wise sage

Why continue crying omniscient one
Upon beholding this beautiful baby
Delivered as a divine sage secretly won
A most magical birth like a sun ruby
Setting on Mount Kailasa joy prophesied
By you pray tell why you sighed
At his transcendent future

Without mocking me foretell the future
Will the prince live long and happy
His fineness unfazed by sorrow's feature
Don't say death will destroy him healthy
Is my fame free from destruction
Is this sacred prize of secure station
Will I be re-born

Dear king don't be mentally disturbed
Fear not friend that he will change
I am powerfully distressed perturbed
That gods deem me soon to die estranged
From this child forever who was born
To clarify spiritually achieving the unborn
Destroying birth itself

Your young wonder will leave his kingdom
With immense indifference to worldly objects
Through continual contemplation he'll fathom
The case of cause effect as knowledge perfects
He'll wander forth ferrying a warming sun
With wisdom compassion his luminous beacons
Destroying worldly illusion

He'll dare deliver the world distressed
Sailing a skiff of knowledge around
Freeing all dejected drained digressed
In oceans of fathomless misery drowned
Tossed tumultuously by waves of old age
With sorrow's sickness a foamy rampage
Advancing dreaded death

The thirsty world will partake the stream
Of his meditative mirror wisdom cool
Embanked by moral measures esteemed
Virtue and vows sweet as twilight lunule
He'll proclaim paths of direct deliverance
For those suffering sorrow's conscience
Entangled in desire's objects

He'll smash asunder the bolted door
Locked by pervasive passion and desire
His timeless teachings will deftly downpour
Putting out attachments to objects like wildfires
The ensuing escape from self delusion taught
New nectar nourishment for travelers caught
Lost on their way

Don't sorrow for a savior son a prince
Dear king but sigh and sorrow greatly
For anguished humans who in illusion wince
From inbred intoxications most awfully
Unaware of golden light liberations's path
Since I cannot pursue Siddhartha's footpath
My spirituality fails

The sage Asita retired riding the wind
Townsfolk tenderly watched him fly
The king's happiness no longer dinned
Aware his son would worldly objects decry
The city celebrated and feasted ten days
Passionate prayers ceremonies did upraise
The radiant prince's fortune

With regal rejoicing heart the king entered

The city with Queen Maya and babe in tow
On a palanquin with elephant tusks armored
With white flowers flashing gems hallowed
The wife and child and king regally ambling
Hailed honored by citizens blissfully beaming
Blessed by immortals

Tai Sheridan

Canto 2: Life in the Palace

A true master of himself one day
His being the end of birth old age
The beneficial influx to the king's cachet
A rising wave of wealth sans gage
Elephants horses fine friends augmented
Fertile milking cows big and bloated
Beyond Suddhodana's desires

Heaven rained on Suddhodana's kingdom
Warm winds blew without hail or thunder
Clouds lightening wreaths in sky's sanctum
Fertile fields the blessed birth did augur
Enemies erasing long-lived animosity
Indifference disdain turning friendly
Companions most endearing

Prosperity pleasantries peace returned
Pregnant women healthy babies bore
All gave work's wealth earned
Mayhem murder were no more
Throughout Kapila families treated kindly
Debts duly paid sans parsimony envy
Harm lying ceased

Heavenly happiness in the palace
Thieving skulduggery scamming ended
Famine fear illness no longer grievous
Lascivious and lustful trysts ceded
Harmonious marriages husbands faithful
Envy greed passé not lingering harmful
All religions respected

Prince Siddhartha the fine king's son
Ten thousand things found their rightful place
Queen Maya joyful with the beautiful burgeon
Yet avoiding death she heavenly flew sans trace
Thus youngest sister Maha Pajapati nourished
The prince lovingly that he be cherished
Like the son of gods

The royal prince grew in pure perfection
A youthful yellow sun on majestic mountains
Like a forest fire in wind fanned cauldron
Like a midnight moon and flying falcon
Townsfolk bestowed gilt-edged gifts upon him
Sandalwood plants ornaments of every whim
A prince indulged

Suddhodana invited entry to eros
Fearfully forgoing Asita's vision
Of the prince's transcendent cosmos
So upon his sensual son good fortune
Bestowing Yasodhara the beautiful bride
A goddess gentle wife near astride
Guile's hopeful blessing

The playful prince received fine pleasures
With dark disturbing thoughts aroused
Reclining among private palace altars
With singing spicy women he caroused
He gazed upon the room's resplendent décor
Female fingers on soft tambourines adored
The palace incandescent

The pampered prince enjoyed life erotic
Garland playmates femmes' sweet voices
Tactile teasing winks and verses graphic
He recklessly pursued pleasure's auras
Delicate nights making love with consorts
Falling from heavenly chariots to cavort
Lost in midair

Suddhodana remained serene settled calm

Devotedly trusting Siddhartha's destiny
The king practicing self restraint sans qualm
Not harming with tongue body mind most ably
With mature means unswayed by pleasures
Aggression minced with mind's measures
Virtue unsurpassable

The king avoided all vexatious acts
Wishing blessings well to mankind
And as the brilliant sun god refracts
Worshiped prayed sacrificed and inclined
To give gold and cows to worthy brahmans
Purifying body and mind thus begins
Self produced calm

The king spoke only kind speech
Citizens and servants followed his way
His blind wrath of heart never in breech
His dealings with others deft fair play
Wisely avoiding attraction and repulsion
Giving away wealth like an almsman
Nobility sans pride

Rahula was born to Yasodhara the fair
The King rejoiced as with the royal prince

Feeling rapturous love beyond compare
The bright ardor of father son that glints
Of heavenly light cast from religious sacrifice
Don't harm living beings was his advice
Brilliant virtue wisdom

The king continued deep abiding calm
Refusing all objects of sensual desire
Kindly holding his kingdom in palm
Tolerating for the prince a worldly empire
His only wish blessings and welfare for all
And to prevent Siddhartha's religious call
Hoping pleasures distracted

All bodhisattvas to fabled forest take
Upon the birth of their first born son
But the prince did for erotica's sake
Evade the destiny of heavenly ensigns
Yet the path of wisdom germinated within
The heart from whence dharma begins
Awaken supreme wisdom

Canto 3: The Prince in the City

Siddhartha delighted in sweetest spring
Green grassy forests lush lotus ponds
The city fragrant a beautiful blossoming
The prince enchanted by unfurling fronds
The king ordered all hide from view sickness
No beggars or lepers or dying or armless
Only beauty's wide road

The king's gaze lingered on his son
The salty tears of love upon his cheek
When the palace prince came down to run
About in golden chariot with hoofed beat
Four gentle horses set upon the road
Purple flowers and banners bestowed
A moon at twilight

The entourage slowly set upon the road
Wide eyed townsfolk awed enamored
Praises for the youth's gentle way echoed
His magnificent appearance well adored
All wished Siddhartha a long happy life
Rich and poor bowed in health or strife
A heavenly auspicious procession

Kapila with celestial nymphs from heaven
Women scantily attired on rooftops above
Bewildered like bird flocks flying brazen
Healthy hips breasts slowing those doves
Swaying in windows with earrings tinkling
Lotus faces bright at the prince's coming
Women falling to earth

Pure women wished his wife happiness
Eyes playing on the prince with reverence
Knowing the statuesque son was dauntless
In devotion to a wisdom path of mergence
One day he'd part from regalia royalty
Though now he knew life naively
Yet a heavenly trick

The gods an aged being manifest
A heavenly upheaval of the prince's heart
As he saw a decrepit man near abreast
No youthful vigor nor vitality to impart
He asked his driver to tell the truth
Of the white haired human so uncouth
With flaccid tone

Is his bearing now natural or accident

To the prince the charioteer replied
Sans harm intended in kind comment
That is old age ravisher of beauty's tide
Vitality's vanquisher and cause of sorrow
Bane of memory end of delight's flow
Enemy of senses

As a child he drank mother's milk
Next youth then virtue and vigor
Now old age's omen his natural ilk
The startled prince asked his driver
Will this evil come to me and all
Why yes indeed with time fate befalls
Even a noble prince

The world knows age's beauty hexed
But upon hearing of nature's harm
The soulful lord's mind sadly vexed
Truth's thunderbolt was old age's alarm
The prince upon the old man gazed
Sighing as sighting with thoughts dazed
He spoke concisely

Saying old age seemingly strikes down all
Memory vitality charming looks wasted

Yet a world not heeding as death befalls
The true condition whence all are headed
Turn back the horses to palace away
I can't enjoy garden pleasures today
Old age overpowers

The prince plodded home in revery
Returning to royal palace forlorn
Happiness lost no longer so carefree
Old age old age old age a true thorn
Once again he asked king's permission
Toward the city he wished to hasten
To view life

Gods downed a diseased man on the road
Suddhodana's son of driver inquired
How this swollen bellied being did erode
To a body pale thin wasting and soured
Shaking slack jawed with wheezing lungs
His shoulders slack a blackened tongue
Calling strangers mother

The charioteer told Siddhartha of sickness
All men become like the wounded wasted
Then asked the prince about this bleakness

Does only this man or do all fall ill aged
His lesson learned that all people fail
Yet many primal pleasure's still inhale
The prince trembled

With sorrow Siddhartha whispered truth
That in the calamity of disease's cacophony
Many smile serenely asleep in untruth
Oh dear charioteer to the palace deftly
Upon the ravages of disease beholding
My mind turns back inward ailing
Repelled by pleasure seeking

The king felt forlorn at his son's appearance
Thus he went to chastise condemn and chide
Officials paving the road's lovely pleasance
Then arranged artful erotic pleasures inside
Hoping the restless prince would not depart
But Siddhartha took no pleasure to heart
In languorous play

Siddhartha readied for a third city saunter
The king from love assigning singing women
To join the prince and with him banter
The royal road again a heavenly vision

Guarded well from vileness and vulgarities
The charioteer ordered only to please
Taking a new road

Gods deposited a dead man on the drive
Which only charioteer and prince perceived
The prince wondered what was being connived
By four men's load by mourners bereaved
Who was this being no longer breathing
To which the driver's mind gods aiding
Spoke the truth

Before us a man with everything lost
His intellect personality breath sight
Like wood straw his earthly time tossed
Sleeping unconscious his fine funeral rites
No enemies or friends abandoned by all
To only this man does this befall
The prince inquired

Death the final demise of living beings
The charioteer clear nobody fools fate
Not dull quick lowly nor kindly kings
The whole world trails through this gate
Siddhartha sank down saddened overwhelmed

And addressing all in clear voice loosened
Over the chariot's side

He pronounced gravely that everything ends
Yet as if blind the world seeks infatuation
A sorrowful state that ignorance pretends
Not letting the heart's composure awaken
Turn back dear charioteer this no place
Or time for pleasure seeking to life deface
Heedlessness facing death

But the charioteer continued straight ahead
To Padmakhooa forest with the Prince
Where intoxicating saplings lotuses red
And gaggles of gorgeous women gave hints
With nymph like and heavenly pleasures
Seducing Suddhodana's son the treasure
In weakened state

Canto 4: Seduction Spurned

Winsome women over the prince drooled
Enchanting eyes hands demurely folded
Their passionate minds around him wooed
His gentleness and majesty well molded
Like scented night's ambrosial moonbeams
Some yawned to swallow the noble dream
Bewitched in silent wonder

The son of priest Udayin in amazement spoke
What fine women so skilled in amorous arts
Each adept at sensuous styles easily invoked
Even arousing sages lacking desire's darts
Ensnaring gods charmed by nymphs of heaven
Their coquetry beauty grace beguiling women
Love's laced ways

I beg of you stop seducing the young prince
That Suddhodana's family may prosper well
One seer succumbed to whore Kaei's hints
Monk Manthalagautama by Blamukhya fell
And wily Oanta the naive Uyaeoiga captivated
Nymph Ghotaca imprisoned Vievamitra mounted
Religious men shamed

The nymphs feeling shot in the heart
At first crazed horrified hysterical
Then they increased their erotic art
Winking flirting smiling golden bangles
Goggling jostling the prince in woods
Lasciviously licking lips as they could
An elephant herd

Siddhartha shone like a sun in royal garden
Beguiling belles pressed their breasts on him
Some went stumbling as smitten maidens
A drunk with luscious ruby lips svelte trim
Whispered a wish from her swelling flower
Another perfumed held his hand in tether
Crying adore us

The youthful maidens carried away by love
Flashing thinly clad hips a saucy beacon
Breasts jingling like jars golden olive
A goddess's sweet song enticing an erection
With finespun flower garlands to flaunt
Catch me if you can a flirtatious taunt
Intoxicated cuckoo songs

The prince restrained his senses well
Without celebration response reaction
He thought 'one must die' the true bell
Calm in contemplation and non action
Sultry women can't see youth fickle
Old aged destroys all beautiful bangles
Their happiness but ignorance

These women know not of death
That descends nor of rampant disease
They frolic in ignorance every breath
Who finely wrought could find ease
Knowing sickness old age death as real
Only one remaining self-possessed is able
To avoid affliction

Udayin said don't demean despise pleasures
Learn oh prince to woo women by flirtations
Treat with reverential compliance these coaxers
Please these wide eyed women's notions
Even if you don't desire amorous frivolity
Your bountiful beauty worthy of courtesy
Support the advantageous

The prince replied with thunder's voice

Though sacred traditions support lovers
With fine friendly words I won't rejoice
I don't despise worldly ways as cankers
While others in worldly objects are stuck
I find no pleasure in passion's havoc
Old age death the real

Pursuing pleasure sense satisfaction is unworthy
Of the wise for beauty passes with old age
You can't approve of passions that blindly
Motivate men trap them in a conditional cage
Anyone knowing they are subject to disease
Old age death who frolics with feminine furies
Is but a bird or beast

Greatness isn't garnered in attachment to objects
Nor within passion's lack of restraint repose
To seduce a woman by guiltless guile injects
Shame as does compliance with woman's woes
Precluding union with one's own natural whole
If driven by attachment or by passions cajoled
Self-deceiving blindness

I'm afraid perturbed bewildered of terrors
Concerning life's disease old age and death

Tai Sheridan

I can't find peace or self-possession's colors
Nor can I find pleasure with each breath
While seeing the world as if ablaze
Only iron hearts wouldn't weep in gaze
Upon great terror death

Prince Siddhartha give a speech of resolve
To end pursuing pleasure's objects of desire
This lord whose eye is worthy and evolved
Left for western mountains to contemplate retire
Then seductresses in garlands left as well
With broken hearts and dreams dispelled
The prince pondered the transitory

Canto 5: Flight From the Palace

The prince didn't yield to passion's way
Lions heart pierced by poisoned arrows
While playing with family friends one day
He longed for forest ease to enclose
Galloping over ground sans king's permission
On fine steed Kauthaka toward golden vision
A moon on a comet's tail

The forest and earth wonders whispered
To him like furrowed fields windswept waves
Dead eggs insects uprooted grass rendered
The prince sorrowful as if family graves
Sighting farmers faces laden with dust's pain
Burnt by sun wind their cattle strained
Potent compassion flowered

Dismounting his steed and struck by sorrow
Wondering of birth destruction he grieved
Longing for ease sweet solitude's plateau
He sat still surrendered against rose-apple tree
Young grass shoots shimmering like lapis lazuli
Lovely leaves trembling in windy abbey
Meditating on origin destruction

The paramount path of stabilized mind appeared
Instantly he was freed of all sorrow woe
No more by desire of objects driven steered
Toward bad deeds mental agitation a letting go
Dwelling in deep contemplation joy bliss
The first realization false duality dismissed
He pondered the world

Sickness old age death such misery abounds
But people by passion blinded as if asleep
Their friends fellows with contempt surround
Upon seeing the condition in which they steep
If I displayed disgust for those subject
To the ravages of sickness old age death
How unworthy my station

The joys of youthful vigor vanished in a moment
The prince neither rejoicing nor remorseful for past
His unhealthy hesitation indolence tiredness went
No hunger hatred derision desires could last
A pure passionless meditation arose within him
Upon which a beggar crawled to touch a limb
And ask Siddhartha

Why oh prince dress in beaten beggar's garb

The sagely strongest bull of men replied
To aspire an ascetic terrified of birth death's barb
Looking for the world's liberation as it collides
With destruction oh I desire the indestructible
abode
Away from all with passions not winnowed
My thoughts unlike others

The beggar then sauntered sans hope family
Far to forests mountains empty homes
Scrounging for food seeking supreme reality
Then suddenly he flew to sapphire sky domes
In truth a high heavenly being come
Perceiving the prince thought as a pilgrim
Not just royalty

The beggar had come to arouse aspiration
And after flying a soaring bird into strata
The prince was astonished joyful well won
Knowing the meaning of the word dharma
He walked the way of deliverance with complete
Freedom like Indra did sense-attachment unseat
Home he rode

Seeking an end to old age death he entered

The city where the princess welcomed him
As husband true yet the prince was calmed
Regally resolved to nirvana's search within
Siddhartha grand like a golden mountain
Eye of bull voice of cloud a lion hidden
A full moon

He asked to depart a meandering mendicant
For love's sake for the liberation of all beings
The shaken king an elephant tree struck vibrant
With tears emoting he entreated no endings
Dear son don't depart to the dharma
Religion is full of evil in youth's karma
Only passions drive

I will leave you my entire earthly kingdom
Suddhodana proffered saying he would depart
For religion leaving you child in royal custom
Your regal religion must by heroism impart
Governance not the blasphemy of leaving me
Forsake your religious resolution for family
Only elders enter forests

In sparrow's soft voice the prince replied
Dearest father if you credibly guarantee four

Things I will not to farthest forest abide
Promise please that I will not die nor
Will disease deplete my birthed body
Nor will old age belittle youth's bounty
Nor misfortune befall

The King thought these requests ridiculous
The prince stood sturdy as Mount Meru
Saying his course a clear centered axis
Don't foil my palace leaving due
Nor keep me from escaping when able
A house on fire separation is inevitable
Dharma requires leaving home

With kindness the king put guards around
His son and pleasurable intoxicating enticements
Preventing the prince from leaving the grounds
So Siddhartha with sorrow entered the lodgments
Wives with dangling earrings swollen breasts
Enraptured adoring with longing's crests
The royal net

The prince's sun shining splendor dispelled
Darkness he sat on golden seat of grandeur
With diamonds the golden candlesticks beheld

Black aloe-wood incense a perfumed liqueur
The nymphs and night music never stirred
Pleasure or delight he remained assured
Seeking bliss of truth

The gods on women cast a sleeping spell
One embraced her drum like a lover lewd
Another from a tree trunk shaken fell
Clothes disheveled breasts loins denude
Consorts drooling in lounging poses
Watering eyes starring straight in gazes
Passion in shambles

The king's son filled with sudden scorn
Aware that alluring women deceive by dress
And men inflate infatuate upon beauty's morn
Oh before succumbing to base passion's excess
If men saw these wanton women on the floor
With repulsive postures most awful abhorred
Romantic folly would end

Siddhartha desperately desired night escape
The listening gods threw open deadlocked doors
The disheartened prince descended agape
En route in agitation through courtyard floor

To stables and Chaudaka his horse's groom
Asking that steed Kauthaka be bridled soon
Ready to attain immortality

All desires depleted settled in calm resolve
He mounted his horse with golden bridle
A steed of strength vigor swiftness above all
A magnificent mane a diamond sapphire satchel
The prince kindly caressed with lotus hands
Oh fly me steed to highest immortal lands
Into reality's liberation

The white winged horse flew into darkened night
High heavenly gates flew open in city silence
The prince parted Suddhodana sans backward sight
Then caroled a cry like a kingly lion's essence
Until I have seen the father shore
Of birth and death I'll return no more
To Kapila city of my youth

Tai Sheridan

Canto 6: Farewell to the Groom

At dawn the noble one neared a hermitage
The trusting deer and does in sweet sleep
The songbirds silent tranquil in forest foliage
The questing prince felt pleasant quiet peace
As if home then dismounting he dearly
Addressed groom Chaudaka saying clearly
All is saved good friend

Although I am finely fixated on my task
You have followed me flying swiftly
In selfless love's light nothing asked
Well willing to carry out wishes freely
You have won my heart enduring
With affection capacity blazing

Devotion plainly proved

Thank you Chaudaka for cheerful kindness
Please take my honored horse back home
Leave me to dwell in forest dream's canvass
Tenderly take a red ruby with which to roam
And by this jewel's power please help King
Suddhodana my father bear grief 's aching

As I destroy old age death

Don't mourn for me as I leave this time
All intimacy and heart's affections pass
And with clear certainty set firmly in mind
On liberation from anguish on separation's morass
Which repeats again and again for all in life
I leave this sorrow behind letting go strife
Tell my son not to mourn

Upon death few heirs might receive merit
Though many may inherit wealth amassed
Although you may think this be a gambit
At a bad time in truth all time is wise repast
For practicing spiritual dharma in the daily
Moments of life a most fragrant flower worthy
I seek supreme good today

Death that great awesome adversary of living
How can one carry confidence through the days
Please tell the king of our unworthy bearing
For through unworthiness all affection flies away
And where affection is lost no sorrow roots
Chaudaka overwhelmed by these tributes
Drowned in grief's tears

Tai Sheridan

Chaudaka said an iron heart would howl
At your determination my own heart
Grieves since fate flung me far and afoul
Packing this pale horse oh how can I part
Back to sorrowing Kapila and the king
Don't abandon him like doctrines damning
Nor your loving second mother

Can you leave queen wife Yasodara devoted
And virtuous yet as well a young son yearning
Are you a coward to royal dignity blinded
Departing your dear son dissolute aching
I beg before you do not bid farewell
At your feet my deepest refuge dwells
My soul burns

Chaudaka while weeping was lost of words
What will the king say if I alone leave here
Oh such unquiet news for queens wizards
How shall I say you seem unworthy or besmear
Your name Siddhartha a sage sans blemish
My heart would be poor penitent peevish
Who would believe

Don't worry Chaudaka change always comes
All beings live subject to birth and death
Even if I didn't leave fine family customs
In pursuit of pure reality's sacred breath
Eventually death will embrace our whole
Leaving behind all abandoned unconsoled
Birds winging away

Relationships like clouds that come and part
The time of intimacy and entwining a dream
Oh how we deceive and deludedly impart
A constancy yet leaves fade in fall's scheme
The same deceit descends when meetings
Among dear friends end with yearnings
Please part sans grief

The noble horse shed tender tears
At which the prince let webbed fingers
Curved in the middlings gently appear
To fondly stroke his steeds silky textures
Saying cry no more Kauthaka I thee commend
As upon your proved horse nature I depend
Carry highborn onward
Siddhartha seized Chaudaka's jeweled sword
Holding the dark blue lotus hilt and blade

He cut off his hair and crown of lords
Tossing them into air above the glade
Like a gray goose into a garnet lake
Then heavenly beings the hair did take
Longing to worship it

The prince removed his royal ornaments
Then felt longing for simple sylvan dress
Thereupon a celestial being in red garments
Approached as a hunter with heart's largess
Asking to exchange his saintly red clothes
With Siddhartha's white muslin disposed
The prince assented

With pleasure the prince put on the robes
While the hunter assumed his heavenly form
Wearing white linen then to heaven arose
As the prince in wonder walked transformed
To the hermitage newly draped in red
His weeping groom alone the forest fled
Lamenting stumbling home

Canto 7: The Penance Grove

With a lion's stride and deer's semblance
In quiet equanimity the prince entered
The rustic hermitage without royal garments
His natural allure the eyes of all captured
The carriage drivers stopped to stare
Wood gathering Brahmans alert aware
Enchanted peacocks warbled

Homage to the saints Siddhartha paid
As sacred cows surrendered milk cream
The arhats were amazed as he portrayed
A noble stature as if lord of gods supreme
The prince personifying a cosmic glory
Lighting woods as if dawning sun lofty
He longed for liberation

The prince inquired of penance practice
Asking hermits what motivates pure
Devotion at which a brahman ageless
Said eating fresh food as old texts inure
Some live like birds on cattle's corn
Some graze on grass like deer at morn
Some like snakes on air

Some say pain is the mainstay of merit
Some win nourishment at stones supping
Some with their teeth grind corn mullet
Some dine on leftovers after others serving
Some with washed wet hair most holy
Sing to sacred sun god Agni warmly
Some live in water

The kings son saw no truth in penance
He deemed it dense with dire pain affliction
And leading merely to heaven's presence
All worlds will be subject to change's action
These hermits hoping to world resign
Simply see better ones of self design
Little is offered here

Penance presumed on desire a lost cause
Without examining the evil detriment
Of the conditioned the mundane the caws
Of death which beings fear each moment
They try to be reborn time after time
But in all self-activity in seeking's pastime
They will drown

People endure misery for reasons many

Some sacrifice for the world's sake
Others for the sake of heaven's aerie
But acting from hope will miss forsake
The mark for in seeking happiness a fall
Into misery and failure though called
To noble spiritual paths

Siddhartha out loud pondered things
Since the mind guides a being's body
Controlling thoughts has merit's wings
But if merit by placing pure food in belly
Is gained then deer also imbue merit's debit
And if by pain one acquires spiritual merit
Then by pleasure too

The prince reflected like a mirror moon
Examining the hermit's penances rites
Then prepared to depart one noon
Having perceived penance with insight
Hermitage dwellers followed anxiously
Saying his arrival had filled the abbey
Don't leave us

Siddhartha said he sought no new birth
He wished to saunter from this wood

With appreciation for hospitality's worth
For affection from the admirably good
Thus honoring sincere religious kin
Seeking the self most supreme within
He delighted openly

The nature of cessation is different
From activity he gently explained
I do not depart caused by any affront
Or from repulsion of any here retained
You are like great sublime sages seeking
Truth in sincere talking and waking
They honored Siddhartha

A Brahman spoke lying in sooty ashes
Tall with tangled hair in tufted wrap
Wearing brambles bark eyes reddish glazes
A thin long nose he rose as if mishap
Water pot in hand saying how brave
And aware of birth's evils young sage
You truly are

You have pondered heaven and liberation
With fine intention to follow freedom's path
Only strong spirits dare battle passion

With full alertness like an enemy's wrath
While those suffering sacrifices penances
Continue as slaves to passion's potence
Wishing for heaven

Since your intention is settled quickly go
To Viudhayokounha where Muni Araoa lives
And has insight into absolute bliss's abode
There to hear the sound of truth's missives
Your heart in hearing Muni may be fond
But I foresee you seeking farther beyond
Rejecting his theory

You will drink the entire emerald ocean
Of the known with your nose of a well-fed
Horse large eyes red lower lip fashioned
With scissor sharp teeth you shall wingspread
Take a teacher's chair on earth never before
Won by saints or learned sages wherefore
The prince departed

Canto 8: Lamentations in the Palace

The grieving groom tried to disperse
His sorrow on the return road back
Home but a single days palace traverse
Took eight with Kauthaka's spirit black
His beauty waning his master gone
The ensemble arrived at Kapila anon
The streets empty

The townsfolk traipsing about sans joy
As if the sun was shrouded in azure sky
Fine summer gardens sorrow destroyed
As the groom and nag wandered nigh
The citizens followed Chaudaka's trail
Bathed in gloom shedding tears pale
Filled with wrath

They heard the king's son set out
To forest wild without his finery
Wearing householder's clothes about
His brilliant body for which the angry
Crowd felt blame so they brashly flew
To the forest prince wishing to rescue
And return him

The women wailed in misery's woe
The King paced the palace distressed
Over his son's solemn vow to forego
His rightful reign and to palace divest
With tender tears the humble groom
Took the horse with his grief abloom
As if the prince died

The sturdy steed wailed a woeful sound
The town horses all sang in syncopation
The people were fooled and dumbfound
Thinking Siddhartha back from bracken
Sorrowing women went wild in delight
Rushing like lightening crackles at night
Out of the palace

Women went dancing with dresses askew
Hair in shambles undergarments soiled
Faces missing makeup their sight untrue
Sans pretty painted toes or earrings coiled
Their limbs brash and bellies exposed
No beguiling girdles no pearls disclosed
Upon bare breasts

Tai Sheridan

Beholding Chaudaka bereft they wept
Like cows abandoned by a brahma bull
The King's first queen Guatama sidestepped
Seeming a fond cow with sad eyes brimful
Of tears she fell flat on the ground slain
Arms outstretched like golden plantain
With trembling leaves

The palace was lit by legions of tears
Despondent women wailing sans breath
Fainting in woe for a prince who endears
Noble women berating in grief's death
Princess Yasodhara spoke tears streaming
Sorrow upon her breasts sighs heaving
Voice choked with feeling

How can heart's true love take flight
Abandoning me helplessly here alone
Only you Chaudaka and the winsome white
Kauthaka have reappeared at palace home
Three friends journeyed from this tomb
Now two how can you weep wicked groom
Dishonorable pitiless man

I blame you bastard for my prince's parting

Wish for a wise enemy rather a foolish friend
A great calamity chancing a family's aching
Pity these sorrowing women who senses suspend
Their sparkling sapphires locked away
Eyes like desolate windows begrimed blasé
And the prince unshaken

Chaudaka artfully answered with sad face
Don't reproach me or the horse kind queen
Nor blame us both with guilt most base
For the lord is gone like a god serene
Though I knew the king's command well
A divine force dragged me down in spell
To follow the prince

As the prince parted the gate by magic
Opened and the horse flew above ground
The dark night was pierced by sun's flick
This was the gods or fate's call to astound
Thousands of city guards fell fast asleep
As the prince and horse most high leaped
Fate dressed him red
Fate carried off Siddhartha's royal crown
Don't assume we are blamable at all
For the horse's hinds and I were drowned

Tai Sheridan

As the prince went where the gods did call
The court and women filled with wonder
At the story of the prince parting yonder
A journey's tale

Queen Guatama hysterically wailed in woe
Should such a hero with long arms lion-gait
Beauty bright as gold voice a base bellow
Should he depart or dwell in a hermitage estate
Two tender feet with webs between toes
Soft like a lotus with a wheel on his sole
Living on hard forest ground

How will his manly body thrive in woods
When by birth deserving a bed on palace roof
He's honored with costly clothes rosewood
Perfumes oh how will he remain alive aloof
In clammy cold horrific heat begging for alms
Sleeping on the bare ground sans qualms
In one cloth rag

King Suddhodana bereft of prince bemoaned
Fate oh brave Kauthaka how could you toss
My shinning son away in wood alone
Take me to him or go yourself to moss

To retrieve him on forest floor for without
Him my life is listless lost in dismal doubt
Plunged into sickness

Go find my prince commanded the king
As the ancestral priest assuaged him
Saying sage Asita announced this wresting
The predetermined power of fate's whim
Quoting that he will never be made to dwell
Contentedly even momentarily in heaven's dell
Nor in emperor's domain

Canto 9: Searching for the Prince

Adviser and priest pursued the prince
To the famed forest hermitage afar
The entourage encamped at provence
Gate of Bhargava's abode among stars
The two humbly bowed in honor's way
Inquiring the means to take away
The king's son

Siddhartha came to escape forever
The fears of old age death upon him
We have honorably come here after
Him to which Bhargava said most grim
The long armed prince left for liberation
To Araoa after apprising that ascetics
Seek their rebirth

The two trudged onward upon seeing
The state of things though exhausted
Then they saw the prince now dressing
Sans adornments his radiance sacred
Sitting a benign king at a tree base
A sun amidst a cloud canopy graced
The priest and advisor approached

The priest asked the prince to ponder
The king's eyes raining tears of loss
Anguished arrows plunged in heart's acre
And that although religious life had crossed
His true path it was inopportune to start
By flying to wild woods set well apart
From princely duty

Though thought and ernest effort appear
The ascetic means of this forest life
They are but cowardly concern I fear
For even householders surmount strife
Attaining true liberation oh don't abandon
Your yearning family find compassion
Come to the city

Care for the drowning Sakya king
Your mother calling for her calf
Your wife a veritable widow aching
You son Rahula return on his behalf
Let their gentle love guide you home
Many religious kings wouldn't roam
Rule and seek simultaneously

Tai Sheridan

The bodhisattva of absolute perfection
Paused to consider all kindness virtue
Then gently spoke he would harken
To sickness old age and death's cue
To leave his family and familiar ways
Knowing all wish that closeness sways
A hero's journey

This present parting would arrive again
So I must honor the heralds of loss
No I haven't caused this grief goodmen
The king in dream-like intimacy tossed
No son or family can cause this sorrow
Ignorance the true source of anguish woe
Loss the way of life

No wise man would cherish sorrow
Or losing a family foremost beloved
But loss the way in mankind's meadow
From when out of womb first shoved
Death the all pervasive truth
My leaving for forest as a youth
Is not ill-timed

Time is inseparable from things formed

The only ill time hungering over objects
Time drags the world into times unformed
But all time wonderful for blissful effects
The king offering his kingdom to me
A noble deed but I'ld be sick in greed
Accepting unhealthy food

How can a wise man in royalty thrive
An ill home illusion amassing anxiety
Owning servants weary and passions alive
The golden palace to me only fire's fury
The victuals and viands seem such poison
Kinship no pleasure all dharma barren
Many kings flee

I now cut the net of home and kin
Freed so the net can't capture again
The advisor hearing what lie within
Was freed from desires and did ken
The regal reasoning of this wise way
Pleased at the prince's resolve displayed
But the time was wrong
Oh dear prince ponder your duty
A father sorrows in old age's arms
Your young mind not insightful amply

Tai Sheridan

Examine wealth duty pleasure's charms
Why welcome an unknown risky result
For a kingship known in which to exult
Birth rebirth unprovable

Grab your good fortune as it flows
If an afterlife arises enjoy it then
But if no new afterlife itself bestows
Sans effort comes liberation to men
Perhaps in the spontaneously arising
World there is no liberation dawning
By our own efforts

In the spontaneity of sentient life
Searching is pointless as some say
Things have inherent nature as wildlife
Good evil existence or none don't obey
Our will for the six senses are fixed
Assuredly any likes dislikes premixed
All arises of its own accord

Nothing can alter the course of pain
Or old age no such thing named will
The fetus spontaneously full form attains
Water quenches fire fire ends water's chill

Elements coalesce to create all things
Thicket's thorns or birds beasts' ravings
Nothing made of our desire

Some say creation from Aevara comes
Some say the cause of action is also
The cause of action's cease or what becomes
Being and being's end is caused by soul
Some say coming into being is effortless
Some say liberation attains through aptness
Who can say

Those looking for liberation will weary
Though the wise promise final freedom
To those using their own efforts ably
O dear youthful prince please fathom
If you love liberation then follow family
Society's set rules to attain this acme
May the king's grief end

Don't be troubled by death's reality
Follow the footsteps of those returning
From forest like king Abaraua carefree
And Rama himself many men well fitting
Illustrious virtuous forsook forest arbor

Tai Sheridan

To return regal to duty's diligent harbor
It is no sin

The king's son spoke simply clearly
Patient and firm in religious resolve
No words explain these issue's aurae
As for things existing or not I must evolve
And determine the deepest truth through
Contemplation quietism asceticism's value
The forest calls

I can't abide by conventional beliefs
Men are the blind leading the blind
Nor can I accept controversial motifs
I know not yet the real truth refined
Good souls sensing joy can toil in vain
The base belittle sans joy in truth plain
Wherein lies answers

Kings coming home broke vital vows
Thus they prove untrustworthy guides
The searing sun will flame and dowse
The high himalayas will erode hillsides
Before I wander home as a worldly man
Ruined wrecked by primal passions' span

Sans truth's knowledge

I will not return to a palatial palace
With my primary purpose unfulfilled
Better to enter a flaming fire's chalice
Said the prince in perfect resolve distilled
The advisor and priest sad in sorrow
Returned to Kapila next misty marrow

Canto 10: King Sreoya Visits

The manly prince passed over the Ganges
Like a beatific brahmin arising to heaven
To the palace RajagOha of peaceful valleys
Rounded by five sacred seals and places earthen
The people peered astonished at his awesome
Face and formidable vow to find freedom
Many followed him

Some placed their palms together
Some bowed with heads bent
Showering him on affection's altar
Paying holy homage as he went
Those in brash bright colored dress
Felt guilty gossipers felt distress
Nobody thought improperly

Sreoya the king of Magadha court
Asked what crowds were witnessing
A courtier said that the prince in escort
Was foretold by brahmans as entering
Supreme wisdom or inheriting the empire
Of the earth the ascetic the splendid sapphire
Of the Sakya king

With clear calm eyes the noble mendicant
Went begging with body mind most graceful
Accepting what was offered then silent
He climbed to a mountain cascade portal
Eating near primitive Paooava forest falls
Lodhra trees and plaintive peacock calls
Mankind's sun shinning

Heroic King Sreoya in veneration visited
The forest beholding the bodhisattva calmly
Meditating as if a mystical mountain founded
Spired peak pure like the moon stately
Emerging elegant on an ephemeral cloud
The prince posed in tranquility avowed
The creation of religion

Sreoya approached in astonishment affection
Asking how the penultimate prince fared
Siddhartha readily reassured his fine fortune
His beautiful body and supple mind bared
The kindly king sat on a black blue rock
Oh prince pray tell why you take stock
In a mendicants life

Tai Sheridan

Your lithe limbs mustn't reside in red
Your honorable hand proffers protection
For servants subjects you're not bred
For holding handouts given they cheapen
Your nature oh if not wishing your
Father's kingdom through love's lure
Please take half of mine

Please prince accept my kingdom graciously
Good prosperity promotes the greatest good
Please win merit wealth pleasure's bounty
Plus love and rest the three main foods
Of mankind's life for when mortal men die
Merit wealth pleasure are no longer nigh
In men's eyes

Meander a mendicant later in life
Enjoy the sense satisfactions now
Practice real religion but first take wife
Youth's vigor the enemy of ethics' vow
Since pleasure is hard to grasp
Seize it now as life's magic asp
Leave fickle youth

If religion a sole aim offer sacrifices

Follow the footsteps of your family
In the highest heavens prayer suffices
Indra Lord of the wind offered many
Saintly sages also said the King
The young Prince bold in his being
Remained a firm mountain

Canto 11: Rejecting Passion

The Magadha King's speech seemed kind
Yet harbored hostility with friendly face
Suddhodana's son with warmest mind
Self possessed pure sans anger's trace
Replied oh friend the lessons you bring
Would work for you or similar kings
My path diverges

Having felt old age and death as fear
I fly to this path longing for liberation
Leaving behind beloved kindred dear
More so must sense attachment be broken
I am less scared of serpents thunderbolts flames
Than of worldly objects fortune and fame
I seek freedom

Passing pleasures the robbers of happiness
Floating empty eerie illusions in the world
Infatuating men's minds with hope's bias
For pleasure's hapless victims hurled
About never happy on heaven or earth
Those thirsty subject to hunger's dearth
Unhappy not satiated

No calamity contends like pleasure's draw
People through delusion devote to objects
If a wise man considers the truthful cause
Of woe and finally fears evil or reflects
Why would he pursue pleasure's falsity
Kings who've conquered keep on staunchly
Vanquishing abroad

Never enough each intones in mind
Who would trust these worldly things
At pleasure's pinnacle dissatisfaction binds
Blame the virtuous and sin some sing
Let the self-restrained end pleasure's grip
Fling man's misery and pleasure's slip
To farthest fathoms

Man intoxicates with pleasure denied
He does deeds that shouldn't be done
Wounded he wanders to misery's wayside
Pleasures require toil yet own one
For they part then return causing sorrow
In truth pleasure only briefly borrowed
From time

Tai Sheridan

Primal pleasures burn like torch of hay
Causing strong thirst when turning toward
Them and when grasping their array
They delude defeat thus most deplored
Beings lacking self-restraint are bitten
In their hearts by shadowy demons
Never finding bliss

Pleasures are like flesh flung away
Famished dogs fighting over food
Skeleton grit of dry bones grey
A snarling serpent of foul mood
They exist as enjoyments in dreams
Covering up compassion's beams
Gone in a moment

Deer are deceived by song to destruction
Insects fly into flaming fire to die
Greedy fish follow iron hooks as bidden
Snatching up a hot coal is pleasure's cry
Attachment to things a terrible toll
The loss of fine friends once extolled
Mayhem misery reign

Pleasure isn't joy as some would say

Doesn't desire really remedy pain
Water for thirst food takes hunger away
A house hinders the sun wind and rain
A bath for bathing a bed simply for sleep
A chair heals standing clothes for heat
Objects remedy pain

No wise man would dare declare
He enjoys delights he remedial deems
All pleasures are as variable as air
I can't call them enjoyable it seems
The conditions producing pleasure's gain
Turn around assuredly becoming pain
The attraction of opposites

The way of kings is confused at best
Since pleasure and pain are mixed
I realize royalty and slavery abreast
Not different for smiles never transfix
On a king nor smarts a slave of constant pain
But a king's campaign must much maintain
Therein great agony

Even after conquering earth's ground
Only one city can serve as decent domicile

Tai Sheridan

Isn't royalty mere labor with others bound
Kings need one royal raiment worthwhile
Just enough eating to hinder hunger
Just one bed one seat few things number
All else pride's possession

If king's things are for satisfaction's sake
I can be sensible and satisfied sans kingdom
If any man is satisfied in the world's wake
Then distinctions indistinguishable in tandem
Those who've attained the auspicious road
To happiness no pleasure can harm or goad
Is it not so

No fine friend I don't go to the forest
Nor refuse a regal offer from desiring
Loftier things since I am no purist
Anyone escaping a sinewy snake biting
Or a torch on fire wouldn't turn back
Only those troubled by envy's lack
Might grasp objects

He who lives on alms not to be pitied
For escaping fears of old age death's mask
Clear calm humility happiness exceed

All pleasures then sans pain he basks
Pity those thirsty when wealth amasses
Privileged hungering for pleasure's urges
I long for true peace

Since fate is so supremely well skilled
In turning the world in wily ways
Why should the wise wait to be killed
Before seeking peace for no one can say
When death as hunter might bludgeon
Disease his arrow old age his weapon
The time is now

No diligence draws me to sacrifice
Nor desire for fine fruit plucked
By causing pain to others excised
A merciful kind man can't construct
Profit for future reward through harm
I don't delight in future birth's charm
Sacrifices unseemly

I bid happiness farewell my friend
For to seer Araoa I travel today
Seeking liberation from passion's rend
Guard the world well as I foray

Tai Sheridan

Guard thy sons royalty and religion
And speak strongly to aggressive actions
Guard like the sun

The lamenting king replied with longing
You hope for desire without hindrance
When you accomplish peace abiding
Please favor me with good guidance
Thereupon the noble prince parted
For Vaievantara hermitage wooded
The king returned home

Canto 12: Visiting King Araoa

Sage Araoa addressed the appealing prince
I am pleased you pursue in youth's prime
Sailing over the sea of human misery since
You have pursued worldly pleasure's pastime
Siddhartha said the sage seemed a light
How might I aptly be delivered upright
from disease old age death

Enchanted by the prince's noble nature
And inquiry into the essence of existing
Araoa turned over tenets in his answer
About mortal existence arising revolving
Through two classes of evolvents and evolute
Also the kuetrajye the soul which imputes
Within the body bred

Evolvents the elements five plus identity
Intellect the unmanifested all combined
Evolutes the intellect senses mind body
External objects then the soul divined
The manifests are things born aging dying
The unmanifested the opposite begging
These the essence

Ignorance desire consequences the causes
Of existence mundane and the mistakes
Of identity confusion fluctuation plus sources
Of false means attachment's heartaches
Indiscrimination and gravitation as well
These the thicket of thought to repel
To attain truth

Mistakes wrong thoughts and acts
Confusion calling objects all the same
Identity a sense of I am I and that
Fluctuation more as if I a real name
Indiscrimination implies the unwise
And the illuminated act kind allies
Thus Araoa advised

Fools entangle external objects
In attachment while gravitation
The misery of me and mine affects
Ignorance advances torpor delusion
Including incarnate birth and death while
Anger and despondency darkness beguile
These classic confusions

A wise man must with right view know

Four things the illuminated unilluminated
The manifest unmanifested are the marrow
When the soul senses these four kindred
Without straightness or quickness assumed
The immortal sphere is assuredly attained
These the tenets

To which the prince asked how one
Studies these sacred things and where
The life of learning leads what is won
Araoa clarified that devotees live aware
As mendicants acting ethically in affairs
Appreciating alms contentment sans airs
Walking the lonely life

Passive to feelings pure in meditations
Satisfied within seeing fear's falsity
Arising from primal passion's bastions
In highest happiness and carefree
In passion's absence he restrains
All the senses and attains maintains
Tranquility of mind

The first stage separated from desires
The second stage no pleasure pain

Tai Sheridan

The third stage ecstatic sans pleasures
The fourth stage abolishing all gained
Next no form itself for real has pleasures
All verily void space in body's clusters
Yet farther fetching

With soul contracted extended everywhere
A nihilist finding nothing ever exists
Flying free a bird unbound in air
He is liberated a Brahman like mists
Without distinctive signs Araoa claimed
The study and life liberation exclaimed
Many manifested this

The prince having heard Araoa's axioms
Rejected his proffered tenets reasonings
Saying that these subtle auspicious theorems
Cannot be the total truth of becomings
For until one actually abandons the soul
From the evolutes and evolvents role
The condition of birth remains

You say the sentient soul is liberated
Yet since some soul lastingly remains
There can be no abandonment granted

The constant triad continues in subtle domains
Some say a clear calm mind harmonized
Imperfections controlled and excised
Is true liberation

Identity is not incapacitated nor gone
As long as soul continues on ahead
Without freedom from qualities foregone
No liberation will be won widespread
Fire flames heat are one sans separation
Before the body exists all is barren
Originally free

First how can a free soul become bound
And if a subtle soul is knowing certainly
Then an object form must be known or found
Existing so soul still is not liberated amply
The prince asserted that absolute attainment
Arrives only in abandonment everything absent
All must go

Unsatisfied the prince went as pilgrim
To Udraka's hermitage and teachings
Of named and non-named beyond Nihilism
Of no named and no non-named deeming

Tai Sheridan

But since something once again returns
The Bodhisattva left on his sojourns
Seeking something beyond

Leaving the hermitage humbly resolved
Seeking final bliss he set out to the city
Of great sage Gaya where he sat involved
With five mendicants in ascetic systems holy
Austerities calming controlling the five senses
The prince thought perhaps this may dispense
Birth and death

For six long years Siddhartha stayed
Practicing self-mortification abstinence
Mortifying for merit until finally strayed
Seeking solace so he might commence
The wished for wisdom's farther shore
He swallowed a few fruits sesame seeds for
His health

Though thin his beauty still bountiful
Bringing gladness as the moon in autumn
Skin and bones the prince shone spectral
His great grander like ocean awesome
Dreading continued existence he considered

That losing strength was assuredly absurd
For pursuing passionlessness

Calm is cultivated by satisfying senses
Meditation requires self-possession rest
The wise seeker of wisdom dispensed
To eat for health and increase vigor zest
Nandabla at the river her heart conjured
In bliss with lotus eyes open offered
The prince milk

With his six senses completely satisfied
He glistened glowed a mirror moon an ocean
The five fasting mendicants left desultory denied
Presuming the prince returned to worldly fountain
Siddhartha strengthened his robust resolve
Invoking intentions to living dying mystery solve
He sat under a holy fig tree

Then Kala the scaled serpent sage majestic
Like awesome elephant lord Ganesh awoke
Spouting praise upon the pure prince cosmic
Assuring attainment of knowledge would evoke
As a flight of fluttering birds offer greeting
As gentle breezes blow in blue sky bristling

Tai Sheridan

Today you will become the Buddha

The prince sublimely sat on his seat
Resolved only to obtain perfect wisdom
Settling his legs limbs body firm complete
Solid like a sleeping serpent's hood become
He said I won't rise from this earthly place
Until my ultimate aim of being is graced
Heavenly beings rejoiced

Canto 13: Mara's Defeat

The whole world rejoiced as the sage
Silently contemplated the highest knowledge
But Mara the enemy of truth did rage
As lord of sense desire his weapons savage
Robust Mara enemy of love and liberation
His three sons confusion pride gaiety all bidden
Three daughters thirst lust delight

Why rage dearest father demanded thirst
Because the Sakya sage sits in resolution's armor
Drawing wisdom's arrow with truth's tip first
Committed to conquer my realms with bodhi's
banner
If he prevails upon this path of total bliss
My realm will wind up empty today dismissed
I must attack

As a swollen spring river assails a dam
Mara seized a sizable flower-made bow
Fetched five infatuating arrows to ram
At the fig tree's foot his children in tow
Then spoke to Siddhartha as he prepared
Crossing to farthest shore formerly declared
The ocean of existence

Tai Sheridan

Hear my counsel clansman afraid of darkness death
Follow your father's duty abandon all liberation
Go gain the wondrous worlds of Indra's breadth
A mendicants meanderings not for royalty bidden
To be king but if you persist I will shoot
This arrow of madness mayhem most acute
You of feeble power

Come quickly to your complete senses
But the Sakya saint stayed calm and firm
Thus Mara shot and six children dispensed
Yet the silent sage gave no heed nor affirmed
Mara sank and spoke that a love arrow aimed
Which had severed saints from vows tamed
Had not harmed

The prince deserves the rebukes and wrath
Of the denizen of demons within my mind
So Mara and all swarmed Siddhartha's path
With arrows darts swords clubs combined
With faces of bears boars camels tigers
Horses elephants fishes assess adders
Tusks claws headless trunks

One-eyed two-faced three-headed monsters
Big bellies speckled bellies blended with goats
Mutilated faces monstrous mouths flayers
Laced in leather naked with trembling throats
Faces half white bodies half green red black
Yellow copper colors jingling rattling attacks
Long serpent arms

Some tall as palm some small as children
Birds with ram's heads cat's crying faces
Hair hanging topknots cawing cretins
To put the prince's mind in clutches
Leaping wildly laughing loudly dancing
Sporting about in scalded sky cavorting
Some on tree tops

High heavens darkened the entire earth shook
As demolishing demons cackled and circled
The base of the Bodhi tree a violent wind took
Stars didn't shine the waxing moon wobbled
The night plunged pitifully into blackness
The auspicious oceans were agitated blueness
The battle raged

The mountain gods and dragon spirits scorned
Mara's deranged destruction of the supreme saint
They kept their compassionate hearts adorned
Without malice they pitied poor Mara's taint
As they saw the assault on the Bodhi tree prince
The sky plumed with pure being's provence
Wanting the world's liberation

The great sage stayed composed and calm
During the onslaught like a lion around oxen
Then Mara directed the demon army maelstrom
To terrify the prince his religious resolve deaden
Sharp savage teeth shaking with tongues hanging
Spiked ears massive mouths gory eyes glaring
Attacking to frighten

One striking with staff was swiftly paralyzed
Some slinging stones tall trees keeled over
Axes and masses of blazing straw outsized
Hung stuck in the sky as shattered vapor
Flaming fireworks of falling embers rained
For Siddhartha's immense charity ingrained
Turned weapons to red lotus-petals
The Sakya saint stayed firm in his posture
And resolve as some spat serpents but

Their venom froze as if by charm's censure
Showers of stones turned to a flower streamlet
Five arrows failed like the five senses of those
Pursuing pleasure's objects or embodiment oppose
Mankind's faults cause failure

Fickle Meghakala flitted about with skull
In hand like students over sacred texts
To infatuate infiltrate the sage's mind artful
But the sage slipped away as do pretexts
For pleasure when truly happy contexts
Are pointed out

A monster heaving heavy rock wearied
Like one finding fatigue as a substitute
For supreme holy happiness ferried
Only by meditation or knowledge astute
All beings were terrorized by Mara's beasts
As if screaming birds bandied about a feast
Thunderbolts bursting heaven

The settled saint didn't flinch or falter
He played with the petrifying phantasms
As if rude children but Mara absent ardor
Attacked in grief and anger's tantrums

Until an invisible pre-eminent beatific being
Upon seeing Mara's malevolent arming
Spoke loudly sans spite

Pause your malevolence and practice peace
You aren't able to shake this sage more than
Wind can mighty Meru mountain crease
Even if fire loses heat or water no more ran
He'll never release his resolution renown
With his clear compassionate heroic crown
He'll stay seated

As rubbing wood starts searing fire
As digging wells finds withheld water
Nothing is unobtainable to acquire
With his perseverance all answers
Will be revealed so don't hinder him
The great physician who works within
For the anguished world

He who patiently pursues the one good path
While the world wanders on devious roads
Should not be shaken for a guide on bypath
Leading a lost caravan must maintain his modes
Don't quench this knowledge lamp or strike

A lamp kindled in gloom oh a living light
For those in darkness

How dare you damage the prince with eyesores
For the dark world drowning in deep floods
Of existence unable to reach father shores
For Siddhartha strives to send over rapids
All suffering beings safely sans illusions snares
Don't raze this tree of knowledge rare
His deep roots firm

His fine fibers patience his flowers a suit
Of moral actions his branches memory
His generosity giving dharma fruit
Today is the time for his actions that agree
To awaken supreme awareness on this seat
The navel of earth's surface complete
This precise spot

He sits in contemplation's home well honored
In worlds of well-being and plentiful peace
O Mara give up grief and wear calm tailored
Pride is improper and fortune unstable caprice
Why posture and pose on a tottering base
Don't let your greatness play in pride's race

Tai Sheridan

Be gone now

Mara listened and looked at the solid sage
Then fled dispirited defeated back broken
His purpose and attacks a ruined rampage
The monsters departed deadened beaten
The passionless sage sat victorious and vital
Having conquered doom's darkness bestial
A fearless sage

The maiden moon and stars shone brightly
A sublime sky soon grew cloudless and clear
Falling flowers from above rained richly
As the wicked one fled the sacred sphere
The Sakya sage with content compassion
No longer subject to Mara's phantasms
Peace reigns

Canto 14: Buddha's Enlightenment

After conquering Mara's hosts most wretched
Using samadhi's steadfastness and tranquility
The bodhisattva became centered concentrated
To awaken clear insight into ultimate reality
The first watch the saint's succession conjured
A panoply of previous births unnumbered
Remarkably recalled

The seeking saint filled with compassion
For all living beings knowing that leaving kin
From this life to the next new one destined
Turns round and round like a wheel spins
His conviction grew that the conditioned cycle
Lacked primary substance as a plantain kernel
He rested resolute

The second watch he who's energy had no peer
With supreme divine eyesight purifying
Witnessed the world as if a spotless mirror
With cultivated compassion for creatures dying
Awake to the law of consequences for should
Someone harm their misery manifested and if good
Then triple heaven arose

Those that harm are reborn terrified
In a dreadful dire horrific realm of hell
Some dwellers drank molten iron inside
Some on hot piercing iron pillar fell
Howling some parboiled in iron cauldrons
Some broiled on red-hot coals crimson
Dogs with iron teeth

Iron crows gloating gnashing iron beaks
Longing for cool shade succulent forests
Some chopped with axes shouting shrieks
Their hatred and harm stopping breath's gusts
Uselessly seeking to end woeful suffering
With pleasures that boomerang back smacking
Tormented retribution

The menace minded pay the price for
Foul acts with loud lamentations when
The terminal hour of retribution in uproar
Arrives amidst these mean men
If they felt the fruit of their foul act
They'd vomit hot blood as if hacked
In vital organs

Unsound minds may be born into beast animal

Realms to be wretchedly slaughtered before
Their relatives for wickedness wantonness carnal
Tormented by hunger thirst fatigue for rancor
If born as oxen horses then poked prodded
If elephants then encroached pummeled pounded
Heads hammered

Stingy people reborn as haunted hungry ghosts
Mouths the size of small needles big bulging bellies
Tortured with thirst hunger and longings utmost
Can't eat filth oh the fruit of avarice's hobbies
Some born from woman's wet womb in human
Realm to suffer at birth when hard hands tighten
A crying child

Loved coddled cherished protected by family
Still demeaned defiled by their deeds done
Fools filled with desire think most unsoundly
They must do this do that as the day runs
Those with much accrued merit born in heavenly
Realms singed by sensual passion's frenzy
Still seeking satiation

Paradise dwellers distressed fall flaming to earth
When heavenly groves lakes left they lament

Tai Sheridan

For paradise is temporal transitory eventually a birth
Lost then separations's suffering ferments
Some surmise paradise is everlasting eternal
Still they miserably fall from celestial steeple
The true world nature

With divine eyesight the prince examined
Life's realms and realized nothing substantial
Exists all empty as a plantain tree opened
Lacking heartwood the cycle of existence lawful
And ever subject to destruction demise death
No peace in the ever wandering world of breath
No resting realm

The third watch of night drew nigh
When the artful adept of concentration
Wondered on what real nature relies
Alas living creatures are born undone
Braving birth growing old passing on
Being reborn an endless cycle anon
Living creatures toil

Mankind's sight surely veiled by passion
And by delusion's darkness beings blind
The creatures so wretchedly cloven

Or lost not fathoming a footpath to find
Out of this great severe suffering
The rounds of realms soundly scathing
People sans peace

The bodhisattva carefully contemplated
The clear causes of reality and existence

Birth causes old age and death created
Like a headache only when a head in existence
   A sequence of acts
Birth properly proceeds from acts created
Not from creator nature or its own existence
   A sequence of acts
The origins of existence in appropriation created
Like vows rules pleasures self views in existence
   A sequence of acts
Appropriation proceeds from thirst created
Like giving birth to passions in existence
   A sequence of acts
Thirst proceeds from sensation created
Like pleasurable taste of water in existence
   A sequence of acts
Sensation proceeds from contact created
Like object sense and mind unite in existence

A sequence of acts
Contact proceeds from six sense organs created
Like the eye seeing an object in existence
A sequence of acts

The sense organs proceed from name and form
created
Like a leaf and stock only when a shoot in existence
A sequence of acts
Name and form proceed from consciousness
created
Like sprout from seed assuming a body in existence
A sequence of acts

The bodhisattva understood the order of causality
Again he contemplated his connected views

As a boat conveys a man so ponder
Consciousness and name-and-form together
Are causes of each other
Consciousness the causal condition
On which name-and-form production based
Yet name-and-form the supporting condition
on which consciousness is also based
Red-hot iron causes a blazing grass condition

And blazing grass on iron red-hot also based
A mutual causality a codependent origination

From consciousness arises name-and-form
  One link to the next
From name-and-form arises senses
  One link to the next
From senses arises contact
  One link to the next
From contact arises sensation
  One link to the next
From sensation arises thirst
  One link to the next
From thirst arises appropriation
  One link to the next
From appropriation arises existence
  One link to the next
From existence arises birth
  One link to the next
From birth arises old age and death
  One link to the next
The world is produced by causal conditions

The bodhisattva then firmly concluded
From the annihilation of birth

Old age and death are suppressed
Take away the basis
From the destruction of existence
Birth itself destroyed
Take away the basis
From the suppression of appropriation
Ceases existence
Take away the basis
From the suppression of thirst
Ceases appropriation
Take away the basis
From suppression of sensation
Ceases thirst
Take away the basis
From suppression of contact
Ceases sensation
Take away the basis
From suppression of sense organs
Ceases contact
Take away the basis
From suppression of name-and-form
Six sense organs destroyed
Take away the basis
From suppression of consciousness
Name-and-form destroyed

Take away the basis
From suppression of all the factors
Consciousness destroyed
Take away the basis

The great seer completely comprehended
That the factors are soundly suppressed
With human ignorance absent and upended
Knowing well what was to be known assessed
Siddhartha stood before the world as the Buddha
Seeing no self anywhere he became a tranquil raja
A fire with fuel burned out

He obtained a perfect peaceful path
Traveled for the sake of ultimate reality
Of which families of supreme seers hath
Cultivated knowing lower higher deeply
At the final fourth watch day's dawn arose
The supreme seer became one who knows
Omniscience and no alteration

As Buddha awoke to wondrous reality
The earth swayed and the sky resounded
With deafening drums the breezes gently
Blew and rain fell from skies unclouded

Tai Sheridan

Unseasonal fruits fell flowers blossomed
Lotuses and golden water lilies welcomed
The Sakya sage

None gave way to anger nor illness
None indulged in mind's intoxications
The world became blessed tranquil wholeness
Deities and beings in lower spheres' dungeons
Rejoiced at the spreading dharma virtue
The world rose above the darkness accrued
By passion and ignorance

All royal great seers filled with joy
At his awakening and from heaven
Revered him invisible beings with joy
Praised proclaimed his pure fortune
The living rejoiced at Buddha's golden
Knowledge but Mara was deadened
Despondent darkened

Buddha sat still for seven days
Sans body discomfort at his ease
Calmly meditating his mind agaze
His heart's deepest desire appeased
Reflecting that on this spot

Was wise liberation wrought
No self nature

The sage who conceived causation
And the natural truth of no-self existing
Filled with great kindness compassion
And with his bright Buddha eye sparkling
Wished for the wide world's tranquility
For wisdom from false views held wrongly
Oh subtle sweet dharma

He resolved to teach the world tranquility
Then two heavenly beings honored him
For the dharma was his companion purely
With wrong doing rejected realized within
Oh sage having crossed beyond the ocean
Of existence rescue the world sadly stricken
Bestow your wisdom

How hard to find a human active
Generous and good for the world's sake
The sage longing to liberate the captive
World grew great and the gods awake
Presented Buddha with four begging bowls
At which four merchants gave first doles

Tai Sheridan

Teaching and generosity one

Wishing to teach tranquility to dispel
Indifference ignorance darkness delusion
As the dawning sun does night dispel
Buddha in Varanasi clarified delusion
Turning his body like an enormous elephant
His sparkling eyes on bodhi tree vibrant
The Buddha Awakened

About The Author

Tai Sheridan

Tai Sheridan was born in 1948 and raised in Southern California. He attended U.C. Berkeley in the sixties, earning a degree in Anthropology and a life based on counter-culture values. A doctorate in Professional Psychology led to careers as a therapist and organizational consultant. He also raised four children in the San Fransisco Bay area.

Tai practiced Zen for fifty years with the Berkeley, San Francisco, and Dharma Eye Zen Centers. After his ordination, he pursued the path of a teacher-writer. He authored The Buddha in Blue Jeans series based on his Zen experience and transformed Buddhist classics into contemplative poetry.

Tai's home studio in Port Townsend looks out at Whidbey Island and the Cascades. He enjoys walking beaches, writing fiction, and sitting quietly at dawn.

Acknowledgments

It took me a lifetime to understand that you are never alone, even on a mountaintop. Since I rely on everything and everybody, I live in profound gratitude.

Bows to my root and ordaining Zen teacher, Sojun Mel Weitsman—you're always near. For Zen training with Roshis Shunryu Suzuki, Sotan Tatsugami, Dainin Katagiri, Jiyu Kennet, Myogen Steve Stucky, and scores of unnamed teachers.

To Berkeley, San Fransisco Zen Centers, Sanghas, and the Shogaku Zen Institute for Zen in the West. For mentors and dear friends Phil Helfaer, Bill Quinn, and Pat Waters.

To my family and friends who hold me to account and keep me in blue jeans. And to all who have loved me.

Books by Tai Sheridan

Anthologies

Buddha in Blue Jeans: Five Book Antholog
Zen Heaven and Hell: A Contemplative Anthology
Plum Blossom Zen: Contemplating Dogen

Buddha in Blue Jeans

A One Hour Short & Sweet Zen Retreat
Buddha in Blue Jeans: An Extremely Short Zen Guide to Being Buddha
Living in Buddha's Three Bodies
Relax, You're Going to Die
Secrets of True Happiness
Zen Prayers For Repairing Your Life

Buddhist Classics in Verse

Celestial Music: Sutras of Emptiness
The Bare Bones Dhammapada: Big Mind Big Love
The Buddhacarita: A Modern Sequel
The Zen Wheel of Life Mantra

Dogen's Zen in Verse

Rice Eyes: Enlightenment in Dogen's Kitchen
Snow Falling in Moonlight: Odes in Praise of Shobogenzo
Warm Zen Practice: A Poetic Version of Bendowa

Contact Tai Sheridan through his website

www.taisheridan.com
tai@taisheridan.com